INFECTION CONTROL

TABLE OF CONTENTS

INTRODUCTION

Infection control is a critical component of healthcare that ensures the safety and well-being of both patients and healthcare providers. As the field of healthcare continues to evolve, the importance of robust infection control measures has never been more evident. The recent global health crises have highlighted the need for comprehensive knowledge and strict adherence to infection control protocols to prevent the spread of infectious diseases.

"Infection Control Mastery: A Comprehensive Guide for Healthcare Providers" is designed to serve as an authoritative resource for healthcare professionals who are committed to mastering the principles and practices of infection control. This book aims to provide a thorough understanding of infection control, covering everything from basic concepts to advanced techniques. Whether you are a seasoned healthcare provider or new to the field, this guide offers valuable insights and practical advice to enhance your infection control practices.

The book begins with an overview of infection control, outlining its significance and the role it plays in healthcare settings. It then delves into the nature of pathogens, exploring the various types of microorganisms that can cause infections and the ways they are transmitted. Understanding these fundamentals is crucial for implementing effective infection control measures. By mastering the principles and practices outlined in this book, you will be better equipped to protect yourself, your patients, and your community from the threat of infectious diseases.

MODULE ONE

LESSON ONE: INFECTION CONTROL

Infection control is the discipline concerned with preventing healthcare-associated infections; a practical (rather than academic) sub-discipline of epidemiology. It is an essential part of the infrastructure of health care. Infection control and hospital epidemiology are akin to public health practice, practiced within the confines of a particular health-care delivery system rather than directed at society as a whole. Infection control addresses factors related to the spread of infections within the healthcare setting, including prevention through hand hygiene, cleaning/disinfection/sterilization, vaccination, surveillance, monitoring/investigation of demonstrated or suspected spread of infection within a particular healthcare setting (surveillance and outbreak investigation), and management (interruption of outbreaks). It is on this basis that infection control and good hygiene are often equated to be the same thing.

The goal of infection control is to reduce the occurrence of infections through a set of practices and procedures known as "infection control measures." These measures include standard precautions (such as hand hygiene and the use of personal protective equipment), transmission-based precautions (such as isolation protocols for patients known or suspected to be infected with communicable diseases), and environmental cleaning and disinfection practices.

Infection control is grounded in several key principles. The first principle is to assume that every person, patient, or healthcare worker is potentially infectious. This approach, known as "standard precautions," applies to all patients regardless of their diagnosis or presumed infection status. Standard precautions include hand hygiene, the use of personal protective equipment (PPE) such as gloves and masks, respiratory hygiene, and safe injection practices.

The second principle involves understanding the modes of transmission of infectious agents. Infections can be transmitted through various routes, including contact (direct or indirect), droplet, airborne, common vehicle, and vector-borne transmission. Identifying the mode of transmission is crucial for implementing appropriate infection control measures.

Contact transmission occurs when infectious agents are transferred from one person to another via direct contact (e.g., touching) or indirect contact (e.g., touching contaminated surfaces). Droplet transmission involves the spread of infectious agents through respiratory droplets expelled during coughing, sneezing, or talking. Airborne transmission occurs when infectious agents are carried on dust particles or small respiratory droplets that remain suspended in the air for extended periods.

The third principle is the implementation of specific infection control measures based on the mode of transmission. For example, contact precautions may include wearing gloves and gowns when handling patients or contaminated materials. Droplet precautions may involve the use of masks and face shields to protect against respiratory droplets. Airborne precautions require specialized ventilation systems and the use of respirators to prevent the inhalation of infectious aerosols.

The effectiveness of infection control measures relies on the commitment and collaboration of healthcare providers. Every healthcare worker, from physicians and nurses to support staff, plays a crucial role in preventing infections. Adherence to infection control practices, ongoing education, and a culture of safety are essential for successful infection control.

MODULE ONE

LESSON ONE: UNDERSTANDING PATHOGENS AND THEIR TRANSMISSION

Infection control begins with a fundamental understanding of the pathogens that cause infectious diseases and the mechanisms by which they are transmitted. Pathogens are microorganisms that can cause disease, and they include bacteria, viruses, fungi, and parasites. Each type of pathogen has unique characteristics and modes of transmission, which determine the appropriate infection control measures needed to prevent their spread.

1. **Bacteria:** Bacteria are single-celled microorganisms that can exist independently, symbiotically (with a host), or parasitically (causing harm to the host). They come in various shapes, including cocci (spherical), bacilli (rod-shaped), and spirilla (spiral-shaped). While many bacteria are harmless or beneficial, pathogenic bacteria can cause a wide range of infections. Common bacterial infections include streptococcal pharyngitis (strep throat), tuberculosis, and urinary tract infections. Bacteria can be transmitted through direct contact, respiratory droplets, contaminated surfaces, and vectors such as insects.

2. **Viruses:** Viruses are smaller than bacteria and require a host cell to replicate. They consist of genetic material (DNA or RNA) enclosed in a protein coat. Viruses cause infections by invading host cells and hijacking their machinery to produce more viruses. Common viral infections include influenza, the common cold,

HIV/AIDS, and COVID-19. Viruses can be transmitted through direct contact, respiratory droplets, airborne particles, contaminated surfaces, and bodily fluids.

3. **Fungi:** Fungi are eukaryotic organisms that include yeasts, molds, and mushrooms. While many fungi are harmless, pathogenic fungi can cause infections, particularly in immunocompromised individuals. Common fungal infections include athlete's foot, candidiasis (yeast infection), and aspergillosis. Fungi can be transmitted through direct contact, contaminated surfaces, and inhalation of fungal spores.

4. **Parasites:** Parasites are organisms that live on or inside a host organism and derive nutrients at the host's expense. Parasites include protozoa, helminths (worms), and ectoparasites (such as lice and mites). Common parasitic infections include malaria, giardiasis, and scabies. Parasites can be transmitted through contaminated food and water, insect bites, and direct contact with infected individuals or contaminated surfaces.

Modes of Transmission:

1. **Contact Transmission:**
   - Direct Contact: Involves direct physical contact between an infected individual and a susceptible host. Examples include touching, kissing, and sexual contact. Direct contact transmission is common in infections like herpes simplex virus and scabies.
   - Indirect Contact: Involves contact with contaminated surfaces or objects (fomites) that have been touched by an infected person. Examples include doorknobs, medical equipment, and shared utensils. Indirect contact transmission is common in infections like norovirus and Clostridium difficile.

2. **Droplet Transmission:** Occurs when respiratory droplets containing infectious agents are expelled from an infected person during coughing, sneezing, talking, or breathing. These droplets can travel short distances (usually up to 6 feet) and infect individuals who come into contact with them. Droplet transmission is common in infections like influenza, pertussis, and COVID-19.

3. **Airborne Transmission:** Involves the spread of infectious agents through airborne particles that remain suspended in the air for extended periods. These particles can be inhaled by susceptible individuals, leading to infection. Airborne transmission is common in infections like tuberculosis, measles, and varicella (chickenpox).

4. **Common Vehicle Transmission:** Involves the spread of infectious agents through contaminated food, water, medications, or medical devices. Common vehicle transmission can lead to outbreaks affecting multiple individuals. Examples include foodborne illnesses like Salmonella and waterborne illnesses like cholera.

5. **Vector-Borne Transmission:** Involves the spread of infectious agents through vectors such as insects or animals. Vectors can carry pathogens from an infected host to a susceptible individual. Vector-borne transmission is common in infections like malaria (transmitted by mosquitoes), Lyme disease (transmitted by ticks), and plague (transmitted by fleas).

Preventing Transmission:

Understanding the modes of transmission is crucial for implementing effective infection control measures. Key strategies for preventing transmission include:

1. **Hand Hygiene:** Proper hand hygiene is the most effective way to prevent the spread of infections.

Healthcare providers should wash their hands with soap and water or use alcohol-based hand sanitizers before and after patient contact, after touching contaminated surfaces, and before performing sterile procedures.

2. **Personal Protective Equipment (PPE):** The appropriate use of PPE, such as gloves, masks, gowns, and eye protection, can protect healthcare providers and patients from exposure to infectious agents. PPE should be used based on the mode of transmission and the type of patient interaction.

3. **Environmental Cleaning and Disinfection**: Regular cleaning and disinfection of surfaces, equipment, and patient care areas are essential to reduce the risk of indirect contact transmission. Healthcare facilities should follow established protocols for cleaning and disinfection, using appropriate disinfectants and contact times.

4. **Isolation Precautions:** Implementing isolation precautions for patients known or suspected to be infected with communicable diseases can prevent the spread of infections. Isolation precautions include contact, droplet, and airborne precautions, depending on the mode of transmission.

5. **Vaccination:** Vaccination is a critical tool for preventing infections and controlling outbreaks. Healthcare providers should stay up-to-date with recommended vaccinations and encourage patients to receive vaccinations for preventable diseases.

6. **Education and Training:** Ongoing education and training for healthcare providers are essential to ensure adherence to infection control practices. Healthcare facilities should provide regular training sessions, updates on new guidelines, and opportunities for professional development in infection control.

MODULE THREE

LESSON ONE: HAND HYGIENE: THE FIRST LINE OF DEFENSE

Hand hygiene is universally acknowledged as the cornerstone of infection control in healthcare settings. It is the single most effective action that healthcare providers can take to prevent the transmission of infectious agents. Despite its simplicity, adherence to hand hygiene practices remains a significant challenge in many healthcare environments. This lesson delves into the critical aspects of hand hygiene, including techniques, products, compliance strategies, and the impact of hand hygiene on patient safety.

Importance of Hand Hygiene:

Hand hygiene is essential for interrupting the transmission of pathogens. Healthcare providers frequently touch patients, medical devices, and surfaces, all of which can harbor infectious agents. Proper hand hygiene significantly reduces the risk of cross-contamination and the spread of infections. Studies have consistently shown that improved hand hygiene practices lead to a reduction in healthcare-associated infections (HAIs).

HAND HYGIENE TECHNIQUES:

There are two primary methods of hand hygiene: handwashing with soap and water, and the use of alcohol-based hand sanitizers. Both methods are effective when performed correctly, but the choice of method depends on the situation.

1. **Handwashing with Soap and Water:**
- When to Use: Handwashing is recommended when hands are visibly soiled, after using the restroom, before eating, and after caring for patients with known or suspected infectious diarrhea (e.g., Clostridium difficile).
- Steps:
i. Wet hands with clean, running water.
ii. Apply enough soap to cover all hand surfaces.
iii. Rub hands together, covering all surfaces, for at least 20 seconds. Pay attention to the backs of hands, between fingers, and under nails.
iv. Rinse hands thoroughly under running water.
v. Dry hands with a clean towel or air dryer.

2. **Alcohol-Based Hand Sanitizers:**
- When to Use: Alcohol-based hand sanitizers are recommended when hands are not visibly soiled and for routine decontamination of hands in healthcare settings.
- Steps:
i. Apply enough product to cover all hand surfaces.
ii. Rub hands together, covering all surfaces, until hands are dry. This should take around 20 seconds.

Types of Hand Hygiene Products:

- Soap: Regular soap and antimicrobial soap are available. While both are effective for handwashing, antimicrobial soap may offer additional protection by reducing transient and resident flora more effectively.
- Alcohol-Based Hand Sanitizers: These are available in various forms, including gels, foams, and liquids. The alcohol concentration should be between 60% and 95% to ensure efficacy.

Compliance Strategies:

Improving hand hygiene compliance among healthcare providers is crucial for effective infection control. Several strategies can enhance compliance:

- Education and Training: Regular training sessions on the importance of hand hygiene, proper techniques, and the impact on patient safety can reinforce the significance of hand hygiene.
- Reminders and Cues: Visual reminders, such as posters and signs near hand hygiene stations, can prompt healthcare providers to perform hand hygiene.
- Accessibility: Placing hand hygiene stations in convenient and high-traffic areas ensures that healthcare providers have easy access to hand hygiene products.
- Leadership Support: Visible and active support from healthcare leadership can foster a culture of safety and emphasize the importance of hand hygiene.
- Monitoring and Feedback: Regular monitoring of hand hygiene compliance and providing feedback to healthcare providers can help identify areas for improvement and encourage adherence.

Impact on Patient Safety:

Hand hygiene is a critical component of patient safety. Healthcare-associated infections (HAIs) can lead to prolonged hospital stays, increased healthcare costs, and higher morbidity and mortality rates. Effective hand hygiene practices can prevent the transmission of infectious agents, reduce the incidence of HAIs, and improve patient outcomes.

MODULE FOUR

LESSON ONE: ENVIRONMENTAL CLEANING AND DISINFECTION

Environmental cleaning and disinfection are critical components of infection control in healthcare settings. Proper cleaning and disinfection practices help eliminate pathogens from surfaces and equipment, reducing the risk of healthcare-associated infections (HAIs). This lesson explores the importance of environmental cleaning, the principles of disinfection, and practical guidelines for maintaining a clean and safe healthcare environment.

Importance of Environmental Cleaning

Surfaces and equipment in healthcare settings can become contaminated with infectious agents, posing a risk to patients and healthcare providers. Pathogens can survive on surfaces for extended periods, making environmental cleaning and disinfection essential for preventing the spread of infections. Effective cleaning and disinfection reduce the bioburden (the number of microorganisms on a surface) and minimize the risk of cross-contamination.

Principles of Disinfection

1. Cleaning Before Disinfection: Cleaning removes organic material (e.g., blood, body fluids) and dirt from surfaces, which can interfere with the effectiveness of disinfectants. It is essential to clean surfaces thoroughly before applying disinfectants.
2. Contact Time: Disinfectants need adequate contact time to kill or inactivate pathogens. Follow the

manufacturer's instructions for the recommended contact time to ensure effective disinfection.

3. **Surface Compatibility:** Use disinfectants that are compatible with the surfaces and materials being cleaned. Some disinfectants can damage certain surfaces or equipment, so it is important to choose appropriate products.

4. **Concentration and Dilution:** Use disinfectants at the correct concentration and dilution as specified by the manufacturer. Incorrect dilution can reduce the effectiveness of the disinfectant or increase the risk of toxicity.

5. **Safety Precautions:** Follow safety guidelines when using disinfectants, including wearing appropriate personal protective equipment (PPE) and ensuring proper ventilation.

Guidelines for Environmental Cleaning and Disinfection:

1. **High-Touch Surfaces:** Focus on cleaning and disinfecting high-touch surfaces, such as doorknobs, light switches, bed rails, and medical equipment, which are frequently touched by healthcare providers and patients.

2. **Patient Care Areas:** Maintain strict cleaning and disinfection protocols in patient care areas, including patient rooms, operating rooms, and intensive care units. Pay special attention to surfaces and equipment that come into direct contact with patients.

3. **Cleaning Agents and Disinfectants:** Use EPA-registered disinfectants that are effective against a broad spectrum of pathogens, including bacteria, viruses, and fungi. Follow the manufacturer's instructions for proper use and dilution.

4. **Cleaning Equipment:** Ensure that cleaning equipment, such as mops, cloths, and brushes, are properly cleaned

and disinfected after each use. Use disposable cleaning supplies when possible to prevent cross-contamination.

5. **Cleaning Frequency:** Establish a regular cleaning schedule based on the risk level of different areas. High-risk areas, such as operating rooms and isolation units, may require more frequent cleaning and disinfection.

6. **Waste Disposal:** Follow proper waste disposal protocols for contaminated materials, including PPE, cleaning supplies, and medical waste. Use designated waste containers and ensure safe handling and disposal.

Challenges and Solutions:

1. **Compliance:** Ensuring compliance with cleaning and disinfection protocols can be challenging. Providing ongoing education and training, conducting regular audits, and giving feedback can help improve compliance.

2. **Resource Constraints:** Limited resources, including staffing and cleaning supplies, can impact the effectiveness of environmental cleaning. Prioritize high-risk areas and high-touch surfaces, and advocate for adequate resources to support infection control efforts.

3. **Emerging Pathogens:** The emergence of new pathogens, such as multidrug-resistant organisms and novel viruses, requires continuous evaluation and adaptation of cleaning and disinfection practices. Stay informed about new guidelines and recommendations from public health authorities.

Impact on Infection Control:

Effective environmental cleaning and disinfection play a crucial role in infection control. By reducing the presence of pathogens on surfaces and equipment, healthcare providers can minimize the risk of HAIs and improve patient safety. Maintaining a clean and sanitary healthcare environment is essential for preventing the spread of infections and ensuring the well-being of patients and healthcare providers.

CONCLUSION

Infection control is a critical aspect of healthcare that demands comprehensive knowledge, diligence, and adherence to best practices. "Infection Control Mastery: A Comprehensive Guide for Healthcare Providers" has aimed to provide healthcare professionals with a thorough understanding of the principles, practices, and strategies essential for effective infection control.

The knowledge and skills gained from this guide are intended to empower healthcare professionals to take proactive measures in infection control. By staying informed about the latest guidelines, continuing education, and engaging in regular training, healthcare providers can ensure that they are well-equipped to face emerging challenges in infection control.

Ultimately, the goal of infection control is to create a safe and healthy environment for both patients and healthcare providers. Through continuous improvement, adherence to best practices, and a commitment to excellence, healthcare professionals can achieve this goal and make a lasting impact on public health.

Thank you for embarking on this journey of infection control mastery. Your dedication to learning and implementing these practices is essential in safeguarding the health and well-being of the communities you serve.

REFERENCES

- Boyce, J. M., & Pittet, D. (2002). *Guideline for Hand Hygiene in Health-Care Settings. Morbidity and Mortality Weekly Report (MMWR).*
- Centers for Disease Control and Prevention (CDC). (2019). *Guideline for Disinfection and Sterilization in Healthcare Facilities, 2008.*
- Centers for Disease Control and Prevention (CDC). (2020). *The Core Elements of Antibiotic Stewardship Programs in Resource-Limited Settings: National and Hospital Levels.*
- Larson, E. (1999). *Skin Hygiene and Infection Prevention: More of the Same or Different Approaches? Clinical Infectious Diseases.*
- Rutala, W. A., & Weber, D. J. (2013). Disinfection, Sterilization, and Control of Hospital Waste. In Mandell, Douglas, and Bennett's Principles and Practice of Infectious Diseases (8th ed.). Elsevier.
- Siegel, J. D., Rhinehart, E., Jackson, M., Chiarello, L., & the Healthcare Infection Control Practices Advisory Committee. (2007). 2007 *Guideline for Isolation Precautions: Preventing Transmission of Infectious Agents in Healthcare Settings. American Journal of Infection Control.*
- Yokoe, D. S., & Classen, D. (2008). *Improving Patient Safety through Infection Control: A New Healthcare Imperative. Infectious Disease Clinics of North America.*
- Zimlichman, E., Henderson, D., Tamir, O., Franz, C., Song, P., Yamin, C. K., ... & Bates, D. W. (2013). *Health Care-Associated Infections: A Meta-Analysis of Costs and Financial Impact on the US Health Care System. JAMA Internal Medicine.*

www.ingramcontent.com/pod-product-compliance
Lightning Source LLC
Chambersburg PA
CBHW071259140726
47996CB00007B/2915